My Breakfast

Diana Noonan

Photography by Lindsay Edwards

This is my breakfast.
It is an egg.

This is my breakfast.
It is toast.

This is my breakfast.
It is rice.

This is my breakfast.
It is porridge.

This is my breakfast.
It is pancakes.

This is my breakfast.
It is hot chocolate.

This is **my** breakfast.

Woof!